Management
In A Minute

The book that delivers practical, proven
and powerful ways to communicate more
successfully and manage more effectively

Created by
Philip C. Cripps

New Generation Publishing

Contents

Let Me Introduce You to This Book

Managing people and communicating with colleagues, friends, customers and clients is never easy. There are so many traps to avoid which is why I have written this book.

My aim is to provide you with dozens of ways in which you can manage more effectively and communicate more successfully.

Each page focuses on one aspect of managing people and communicating with those you wish to inform, advise, influence and persuade.

You can dip in and out of the book. There is no sequence you need to follow.

Seek out the techniques and approaches that will help you to enjoy and succeed, even more often, when you manage and communicate with people.

Philip C. Cripps

Communicating
Your Message
Effectively

How often do you find yourself saying *"YES, BUT..."* to colleagues and customers when they put forward their ideas, thoughts and suggestions? If you express the phrase frequently then here is my message...

"YES, BUT..." is really you saying *"Yes, NO you are wrong".* It's a contradiction in terms. In addition the phrase is often delivered like a verbal head butt!

Make the following change to your vocabulary and you will be delighted with the result. Replace *"YES, BUT..."* with *"YES, AND..."*

Here are some examples of making the change from *"YES, BUT..."* to *"YES, AND..."*

"Yes, BUT that will never work."	*"Yes, AND how will that work for us?"*
"Yes, BUT we tried that last year."	*"Yes, AND how can we do that more effectively this year?"*
"Yes, BUT that would be very expensive."	*"Yes, AND how will we ensure we get the right return on any investment?"*

"YES, AND..." encourages people to say more, to explain their thoughts and justify their views. There is no criticism just encouragement. If the person has not thought through their idea or suggestion carefully, then the individual has the opportunity to think again or withdraw their comment without losing face.

THE *"WHY"* WORD

Business people spend a considerable amount of their time asking others questions. They seek information, opinions, clarifications and reactions. However, what they should not do is create annoyance or irritation. And yet one small word can prove to be the destroyer of a conversation. I am referring to the *"WHY"* word.

"WHY" has been described as the most provocative word in the English language. It has an ability to put people on the defensive. Because when it is used it can, and often does, appear to be a criticism of the person to whom it is posed.

If you want to stimulate discussion, and ensure the people with whom you speak are happy to answer your question, delete the word *"WHY"* from your vocabulary.

Prefix your questions with *"WHAT"* or *"HOW"* and pose them in a relaxed manner. You will generate productive discussions and secure the maximum information in the minimum time.

ARE YOU A "WHY NOT" PERSON?

One aspect of our communication with others is that of putting forward ideas and suggestions. Prior to presenting our ideas we may spend a lot of time evaluating their merits. However, we can put all that hard work at risk by presenting our suggestions in a manner which undermines their worth.

How often have you heard yourself or others introduce an idea with the question:

"Why don't we..."
"Why not try..."
"Why can't we be..."

We are asking a question in a way which encourages the recipients to come up with reasons for rejecting our idea.

Every negative question reduces your chances of success. Therefore, delete the *"why not"*, *"why don't"* and *"why can't"* expressions from your vocabulary. Present your ideas with confidence. Here are some examples. Instead of saying *"Why don't we..."* say, *"Let's adopt this idea..."* and instead of *"Why can't we be..."* say, *"We can make this happen"*.

HOW NEGATIVE IS YOUR COMMUNICATION?

We all have to influence and persuade others during our life. However, we often fail because we communicate NEGATIVELY rather than positively.

How many of the words and phrases shown below creep into your vocabulary?

"Hopefully"   "Perhaps"
"Maybe"   "Possibly"
"You may not agree"
"I'm not sure this will work"
"You may disagree with me, but..."

Each word and phrase reduces the effectiveness of your communication, because it puts DOUBT in your contact's mind. After all, if you do not sound confident, why should your contacts follow your suggestion, advice or recommendation.

With all bad communication habits there is only one action you need to take – DROP IT!

HOW HONEST ARE YOU?

Have you noticed how many people use the phrase *"TO BE HONEST"*. Are the users trying to justify something they have said or haven't they been honest up to the point when they use the phrase?

The phrase *"TO BE HONEST"* can suggest the complete opposite and there is no doubt it encourages the recipient to be on their guard.

So drop it from your vocabulary. Yes, drop it completely. Do not allow yourself to fall into the trap of replacing "To be honest" with:

"To be perfectly honest..."
"To be totally honest..."
"To be completely honest..."
"To be absolutely honest..."
"I'd like to be honest..."
"If I am honest..."

ADD THE POWER OF THE ADJECTIVE TO YOUR VOCABULARY

All too often we fail to give sufficient thought to our choice of words when we speak or write. This is especially true when we wish to enthuse, encourage and influence peoples' attitude and behaviour.

Look at how the introduction of an ADJECTIVE can enhance your communication:

Without an ADJECTIVE	With ADJECTIVE included
"I would like us to make some changes."	*"I would like us to make some HIGHLY BENEFICIAL changes."*
"I am looking for your ideas."	*"I am seeking your CREATIVE ideas."*
"We need new people for the team."	*"We need EXCEPTIONAL new people for the team."*
"That could work."	*"That could work BRILLIANTLY."*

It's amazing what just ONE WORD can achieve.

Adjectives need to be used sparingly, because if you over use them, you can convey the impression of being patronising or insincere.

DO YOU KNOW HOW TO USE "CONDITIONED COMMUNICATION PHRASES"?

Persuading someone to want to do what you want them to do is always helped if you can ensure your contact NODS REGULARLY IN AGREEMENT with the things you are discussing.

Once your contact starts to nod regularly, they become CONDITIONED and, therefore, less likely to shake their head in disagreement.

Conditioning phrases can include:

"As you said..."
"You have always emphasised..."
"Earlier in our meeting you said..."
"I know how important that is to you..."
"You've often remarked that..."

Conditioning phrases need to be used sparingly. If you use them too frequently, your contact may consider them to be contrived.

FAVOURITE PHRASES

Some people speak because they have something valuable to say, while others speak because they have to say something.

People in the latter category often fill their conversations with words and phrases that add nothing to their message, they use FAVOURITE PHRASES such as:

"At this point in time..."
"At the end of the day..."
"When all is said and done..."
"You know where I'm coming from..."
"You know what I mean..."

The favourite phrases generate mental indigestion for the person with whom you are speaking. They also extend unnecessarily each conversation.

Once you remove your favourite phrase you may feel concerned about the silence generated. Don't be. Let the person with whom you are speaking digest the points you have raised. Their response will be a more considered one if they are not bombarded with unnecessary words.

SECURING THE MAXIMUM INFORMATION IN THE MINIMUM TIME.

Think about the amount of time you spend asking other people QUESTIONS. It's a lot.

You seek information, advice, views, opinions, feedback, reactions and ideas. The speed at which that information is obtained, and the amount of information you gain, is dependent upon how you STRUCTURE your questions.

You need to ask questions that are always prefixed with WHAT, WHO, HOW, WHERE, WHEN or TO WHAT EXTENT/ DEGREE.

You need to eliminate the following prefix from your information gathering vocabulary:

- Do you
- Are you
- Would you
- Have you

- Could you
- Can you
- Did you
- Will you

Each of these prefix can, and so often does, generate a *"Yes"* or *"No"* response.

Once you have chosen the right prefix for your question you need to ask it in a manner which does not make it sound like an inquisition or criticism. This can be achieved by using CONVERSATIONAL PRELUDES.

A *"Conversational Prelude"* is a phrase which explains the reason for your question and also encourages your contact to respond. To construct each "conversational prelude", think about how you would like to be asked the question.

HOW EFFECTIVELY DO YOU ANSWER PEOPLES' QUESTIONS?

If you have spent time listening to how people talk with one another you will have discovered how many, when asked a question, demonstrate an inclination to give an immediate response. This can prove to be a significant communication trap, because a hasty and ill-considered response could lead to challenges or confrontation.

You can avoid this communication trap by always using my FIVE STAGE APPROACH©

Stage One: Never answer a question until you are sure you understand its MEANING.
If you are not sure you understand what you are being asked RESTATE the question.

Stage Two: Never answer a question until you know your contact's MOTIVE for asking it.
When your contact does not declare, or indicate, their motive for asking their question use, in a relaxed manner, the REVERSE QUESTIONING TECHNIQUE.

"*What prompts you to ask...?*"
"*What's led you to raise...?*"
"*What's prompted your interest in...?*"

You need to secure a "Because..." response from your contact.

Stage Three: Never answer a question until you have established the level of IMPORTANCE your questioner attaches to the issue.
Your contact may indicate this by means of their intonation. However, when you have doubts ask:

"How important is this matter to you?"
or, *"What importance do you attach to...?"*

Stage Four: Always consider the TIMING of your response.

You may need time to consider the content of your response or you may need to gather more information to enable you to provide a complete answer. Never be tempted to provide half an answer. Confirm to your contact when you will provide a reply.

Stage Five: Always consider WHERE you will or should respond to a question.

The location of your response can have a considerable influence on your contact's attitude.
Private questions should never be answered in public locations.

"STATEMENTS CREATE CONFRONTATION. QUESTIONS STIMULATE COMMUNICATION"

Both business and personal relationships are often compromised by one or both parties resorting to making STATEMENTS. A statement is an expression of opinion and, while opinions are valued, when they are asked for, they can stimulate very negative reactions when they are not.

When you recognise you are about to express a statement, consider how it can be turned into a QUESTION. For example, instead of saying *"I think..."* ask *"What is your opinion?"* Or instead of telling someone, *"You should...."* ask: *"How do you think this can be undertaken successfully?"*

Delete the following statements from your vocabulary:

"I think..."
"I feel..."
"I consider..."
"I believe..."
"In my opinion..."
"I know..."

You will be delighted by the positive impact your move away from STATEMENTS to QUESTIONS will have on your relationship with both your business and personal contacts.

TO ASSUME MAKES AN ASS OF U AND ME

In business meetings and group discussions you often hear the phrases:

"I think we can assume..."
"It's a pretty safe assumption..."
"I'm assuming..."
"Let's assume..."

The reality is that all assumptions are dangerous ones, because they can make an ASS of U and ME.

Assumptions are made when facts are, or evidence and information is, not made available. Therefore, whenever you find yourself in a situation where you need to decide and/or act upon something where the facts, information or evidence is not available ASK STRUCTURED QUESTIONS. These are questions prefixed with *"What"*, *"Who"*, *"How"*, *"Where"* and *"When"*. The prefix ensure the person with whom you are speaking cannot say *"Yes"* or *"No"*. You need to investigate further and test the assumption you are being tempted to make.

If your questions do not provide you with sufficient information on which to give a considered response, then don't be rushed to make any decision.

If you do, it could become a case of *"act in haste, repent at leisure"*.

WHOSE OPINION COUNTS?

When you are communicating with others it can be highly tempting to express your OPINION when it has not been requested.

Of course, we all have views, ideas, thoughts and opinions. But if you have not been asked for your opinion resist the temptation of expressing it. Instead, ask the people with whom you are communicating to express theirs.

By conveying an INTEREST IN those with whom you are communicating you create an environment in which your opinion will be welcomed more readily.

People who readily express their unasked for opinion often believe they will convince others by being INTERESTING. The reality is that you will win more approval from others when you show an INTEREST IN those people.

DOES YOUR BODY LANGUAGE CONTRADICT THE WORDS YOU SAY?

The effectiveness of our communication is determined primarily by our choice of words, our intonation, our ability to listen, our observation skills, and our BODY LANGUAGE.

We need to ensure that our positive verbal communication is complemented by positive body language. This involves us demonstrating such actions as:

- Nodding in agreement
- Maintaining eye contact
- Taking notes
- Smiling
- Leaning slightly forward towards our contact

And avoiding such actions as:

- Keeping our arms crossed
- Adopting a permanently reclined position when sitting
- Doodling
- Tapping the table
- Pointing with a pen
- Frowning continuously

Our body language often speaks far louder than the words we say. Therefore, always make a conscious effort to synchronise your words with your actions.

DO YOU RECOGNISE THE BODY LANGUAGE USED BY THE PEOPLE WITH WHOM YOU COMMUNICATE?

Whenever you communicate – face to face – with others, it is vital to OBSERVE your contact's body language.

You should be looking for a *"CLUSTER OF MOVEMENTS"*. A cluster is three or more related movements, made by your contact, which deliver a message. This message may differ from what your contact has been saying.

For example your contact may say, *"Yes interesting, carry on."* They appear to be supportive of your idea, recommendation or suggestion. However, if they sit back in their chair, cross their legs, cross their arms and look away from you, then they may have some reservations or concerns. The strength of the signals need to be tested with a structured question, such as:

      "What's caught your interest?"
Or,   *"What's your view on the idea?"*

If the response is a negative one then you need to change your approach, or idea, or suggestion to reflect accurately their interests.

EARS OPEN – EYES SHUT

I am always delighted when a person I have coached, over a period of time, comes to me and says:

"I have really benefitted from following your active listening suggestions."

However, what I often find is that an improvement in listening skills is not always followed by an enhancement of an individual's OBSERVATION skills.

Whenever you communicate with someone you need to observe the environment in which the communication is taking place. What messages are the surroundings delivering to you?

Professional Buyers love to use their surroundings to achieve a variety of outcomes. They may wish to intimidate sales people, mislead others, create an impression of total interest or give nothing away.

You need to test your observation skills by asking questions in a relaxed, rather than defensive or concerned manner.

If you do not ask questions you will be tempted to make assumptions. Those assumptions could be completely wrong and result in the creation of embarrassing situations.

Remember to follow this sequence:
- OBSERVE
- ANALYSE
- ASK
- EVALUATE
- RESPOND

TREAT SILENCE AS AN ALLY AND NOT AN ENEMY

If you listen attentively to people you will hear how many feel they have to fill any silence that might feature in their conversations with **VERBAL STUFFERS**.

Verbal stuffers are words or phrases such as:

"Basically" "Actually"   *"Er"*
"Obviously" "Totally"   *"Um"*
"So"   *"Like"*   *"OK"*
"You know" "Absolutely"

Each word or phrase adds nothing to a conversation. However, what it can do is cause severe irritation to the recipient.

If you have fallen into the trap of using consistently one of the words or phrases shown above, then let me explain how to eliminate them from your vocabulary.

1. Slow down your conversation by at least ten per cent. By just touching the brake on your conversation you will give yourself time to structure a positive dialogue.
2. Do not drop your voice at the end of a sentence, because when you start the next sentence, you will be tempted to use one of those negative words or phrases.
3. Create silence gaps. Allow your listener to digest what you have said.
4. Rehearse the words you wish to use during important conversations.

5. Record your rehearsals. When you play back your recording count the number of verbal stuffers you have used and the one that is repeated most.
6. Where possible take notes during conversations.

Silence isn't your enemy. It can be a great ally. Don't be afraid of silence. Turn it to your advantage.

DO YOU RECOGNISE AND RELATE TO THE DIFFERENT CHARACTERISTICS OF THE PEOPLE WITH WHOM YOU COMMUNICATE?

Successful influencers, persuaders and informers know how vital it is to REFLECT the attitudes, interests and behaviours of the people they meet.

REFLECTING involves assessing peoples' interests and behaviour.

Whilst it is dangerous to attach labels to people, it is possible to recognise that individuals can fall into specific behavioural groups. I have named three of the most notable groups: DRIVERS, PROTECTORS and CARERS.

DRIVERS are:

- action orientated
- focused on results/goals
- influencers and persuaders
- prepared to take risks
- motivated by challenges
- competitive
- leaders
- quick to decide and (often) to act
- individuals with short attention spans

PROTECTORS are:

- analytical
- detail focused
- thorough
- often pedantic
- cautious
- practical
- often slow to decide and act

and CARERS are:

- concerned about others views, opinions and welfare
- trusting
- helpful
- supportive
- often reluctant to make decisions

When you have assessed the interests and primary behaviour patterns of your contact, your actions, whether verbal, visual or written, need to reflect their interests and behaviour. DRIVERS require you to be concise. They want to know what they will **gain** from taking your advice or accepting your recommendation.

PROTECTORS need you to be thorough. You need to dot every "I" and cross every "t". Be prepared to give them lots of time.

CARERS need to be assured that the people with whom they are required to communicate will benefit from what you are recommending.

DO YOU LISTEN TO OTHERS OR SIMPLY HEAR WHAT THEY SAY?

Listening and hearing are not the same thing. Hearing is an instinctive act. We do not need to think to hear. Listening is a conscious act. It requires us to undertake a number of very specific actions.

When you are listening you do **NOT** do the following:

- Interrupt.
- Jump to conclusions.
- Allow your prejudices to prevail.
- Focus on the messenger rather than the message.
- Day dream.

Instead you:

- Remain passive.
- Ask questions for clarification.
- Demonstrate empathy with your contact.
- Show attentive posture.
- Smile in agreement and to acknowledge points.
- Convey an interesting tone of voice.

Because, there is nothing you can possibly say to an individual that would be half as interesting to **THEM** as the things they would love to tell you about themself and their idea.

DO YOU LISTEN FOR WHAT PEOPLE DON'T SAY?

Wouldn't it be great if everyone said what they really think and feel? Perhaps not. Because straight and direct talk can offend and upset others. Even when we do not agree with someone we can be tempted to mask our real feelings. We do this by delivering HIDDEN MESSAGES within our responses and conversations.

The skill we all need to develop is that of recognising and responding, in a relaxed manner, to those hidden messages.

Look at the responses shown below. What could they be hiding?

"I quite like your idea." (But you are not enthusiastic or convinced?)
"There's some merit in that approach." (But you also have doubts about it?)
"I'd like to think that would work." (But you're not convinced it will?)
"That's one way of looking at it." (And what's another?)

When you suspect feelings, views and opinions are being hidden, ask a question that is constructed positively. Test that potential assumption.

You will never influence or persuade anyone to want to do what you want them to do until you have addressed their hidden concerns. Let's take the responses shown above and consider the questions you can ask...

RESPONSE	**YOUR QUESTION**
"I quite like your idea."	*"Which particular aspects appeal to you?"*
"There's some merit in that approach."	*"What specific benefits can you see resulting from adopting the approach?"*
"I'd like to think that would work."	*"What results should we expect to achieve?"*
"That's one way of looking at it."	*"What alternative approaches could we use?"*

It is essential to ask POSITIVE questions. Do not go looking for problems which may not be there.

THE "WE" WORD

When your job involves you influencing and persuading people who work within companies and organisations, you know how important it is to be talking to the person with the authority to say *"Yes"* to your ideas and proposals. However, some people seek to hide their lack of authority. Their reasons can include the fear of embarrassment and the desire to appear more important than they really are.

One of the masking devices used by people without authority is the word *"WE".* It is such a small word that it is easy to miss. Nonetheless, if you are an active listener you will recognise when it is being used repeatedly. When it is used frequently listen for such qualifying phrases as *"We at (Company/business name)"* and *"As a business we always..."*

If it is used without a precise qualifying phrase you need to ask a question to establish who else is involved in the decision making. Here are some examples of the questions you can pose:

"Clearly what we have been discussing has caught your interest. With that in mind, who, apart from yourself, will take an active interest in the subject?"

Or,

"I'm glad to hear you like the ideas. Naturally, in a company like your own there are bound to be a number of people who will be interested in the proposals. Who in particular?"

Each question has to be posed in a relaxed manner.

Once a name is (or names are) revealed, establish the role of the person and their likely attitudes/views by asking such questions as:

"What is Mr Jones' role within your company?"
"On what particular issues would he focus?"
"How familiar is he with the topic we have been discussing?"

Follow this up with the positive question of:

"When we meet Mr Jones, would you like to describe the ideas/proposals or shall I?"

The communication sequence I have given you will save you time and increase substantially your chances of securing the agreement you seek.

HARNESSING THE POWER OF "YES"

Every time you communicate with your team members, colleagues and friends, you have the opportunity to influence the attitudes of each person. Therefore, you always need to give careful consideration to your wording and your tone of voice when you communicate.

One of the most powerful ways of engaging and enthusing others is to ensure the word *"YES"* features strongly in your vocabulary.

By adding the word *"YES"* to your dialogue you provide a positive reinforcement. Look at the examples shown below:

"YES, that really went well for you."
"YES, that was a difficult situation, which you tackled with great confidence."
"YES, you have really mastered that technique."

You will notice that the word *"YES"* features at the beginning of each of the feedback statements. The positioning is important as is the tone of voice with which it is expressed. It needs to be an emphasised and not passive delivery.

WHEN IS AN "OBJECTION" NO MORE THAN A RESISTANCE?

When you put forward ideas and proposals to colleagues, team members, customers and clients, you are bound to generate some resistance. However, a resistance is not the same as an objection.

It is human nature to resist change, even when the benefits are clear. But you do not need to challenge a resistance, you can handle it in a positive way through using my DIGGING TECHNIQUES©

A Digging Technique© is a means of testing the strength of a resistance. This is how it works:

- Listen to how your contact raises their resistance. Is it raised in a calm rather than hostile manner? The tone of voice is a great indicator of the importance your contact attaches to their resistance.
- If the tone of voice is not hostile turn the resistance round by using a question. . Here is an example:

YOUR CONTACT: *"I'm not sure that approach will work."*
YOU: *"I can understand your reservations. If I can show you where it has been used successfully in other companies, what then?"*
YOUR CONTACT: *"Well even if you can, the timing's not right"*
YOU: *"The timing of the change is an important factor and if I can highlight the benefits of implementing it now, what then?"*
YOUR CONTACT: *"Then I'd support you."*

Two resistances were addressed. No challenge was made and your contact's concerns were removed, because the DIGGING TECHNIQUE© addressed their need for reassurance.

You will have noticed the use of the phrase: *"WHAT THEN?"* It is used to stop you adding such negative endings to your questions as:

"Would that be OK?"
"Do you agree?"
"Are you happy now?"

However, when you are comfortable using Digging Techniques© you can drop the *"what then"* phrase. Instead, pose your question and raise your voice slightly at the end of the question. This encourages your contact to reply.

You will find that using Digging Techniques© will save you time, effort, frustration and will enable you to influence people more effectively.

DO YOU LOOK UPON PEOPLES' OBJECTIONS TO YOUR IDEAS AS OBSTACLES OR OPPORTUNITIES?

It is rare for any of us to put forward ideas, suggestions or proposals, to those we wish to persuade, which are accepted without questions or objections. When the latter are received there is a temptation to confront the barrier. The phrase *"Yes, but..."* can find its way back into our vocabulary.

Well there is a more subtle and effective way to handle the objections expressed by those you seek to persuade.

Use my A.A.C.© approach.

A.A.C.© refers to Accept Agree and Capitalise.

The approach is based upon the psychology of doing the opposite of what your contact expects you to do.
Here is how to use A.A.C.©

ACCEPT the objection; at least notionally. The last thing your contact expects you to do is accept the existence and relevance of their objection.
Use such phrases as *"Thank you for raising that issue"* or *"I appreciate you asking about"* or *"I can understand you having those thoughts"*.

AGREE with your contact that their concern needs to be addressed.
Use such phrases as, *"I agree we need to discuss this issue further"* or *"I agree that matter needs to be discussed"*.

31

CAPITALISE on the subject raised by your contact by turning the negative issue into a positive one. Use such phrases as, *"Your raising that matter gives me the opportunity to describe how..."* or *"Let me show you how..."*

Here's an example of A.A.C.© in practice.

YOUR CONTACT: *"Your prices are far too high."*

YOU: *Thank you for raising the issue of our prices."* (ACCEPT)
"I agree we should discuss the matter further." (AGREE)
"In fact your raising the subject gives me the opportunity to explain about how we arrived at the prices and the value we can deliver." (CAPITALISE)

A.A.C.© enables you to open the dialogue, to explore what has prompted your contact to raise their objection and to provide further information which will enable your contact to make a considered decision.

The success you will achieve with the A.A.C.© approach highlights that influencing others is achieved through consultation and collaboration and not confrontation.

ARE YOU QUICK TO AGREE OTHERS DEMANDS?

If you are a business person, who has to influence and persuade others you will be very aware that your ideas and proposals often stimulate your contacts to make **DEMANDS**. When this happens, and regardless of the nature and motivation for the demand, you may be tempted to agree to the demand. To some extent this is understandable. After all, you do want an agreement.

On the other hand agreeing immediately to the demand (or "request" as your contact may term it) could have numerous negative consequences.

To protect yourself from these potential consequences add the phrase:

"IT DEPENDS"
To your vocabulary.

You use the phrase like this:

DEMAND	RESPONSE
"Are you prepared to change your price?"	*"IT DEPENDS upon other factors we need to discuss."*
"You can do that for free."	*"IT DEPENDS upon the size and scope of the overall agreement."*
"You want to get this order, don't you?"	*"IT DEPENDS upon the terms and conditions associated with the order."*

33

Your use of *"IT DEPENDS"* conveys clearly to your contact that you are not going to acquiesce to pressure. It also demonstrates to him you are prepared to consider negotiating. However, there is a limit to how many times you can use the phrase *"IT DEPENDS"*.

If you use it more than two or three times during a discussion you will annoy your contact and they may close down the conversation. Therefore, use the power of the word *"IF"* as described on the next page.

ADD THE WORD "IF" TO YOUR NEGOTIATIONS WITH YOUR CUSTOMERS, COLLEAGUES OR FAMILY

We all like to please – don't we?

Well most of us do when it comes to maintaining great relationships with others. However, the action of pleasing others can also encourage us to say *"YES"* too often. Therein lies a danger.

You will have read my message on how and when to use the phrase *"IT DEPENDS"* during formal or informal negotiations. You will also have noted that I recommended using the phrase sparingly. Therefore, what do you do when you cannot use *"It depends"* again?

The answer is to respond to your contact's request or demand with the word *"IF"*.

"IF" makes your response conditional. You are indicating that you could agree to your contact's request or demand provided you obtain something in return.

For example:.

> *"If we were to reduce our prices we would require a two year contract."*

Or

> *"If we were to include that within our proposal we would need your agreement today."*

The use of *"IF"* places the ball firmly in your contact's court. They have to consider whether to accept the condition you have attached to your offer.

"IF" may be a very small word. Nonetheless, you will find it has big protective powers.

SELF-PRAISE IS NO RECOMMENDATION

Have you noticed how many people try to influence others with the phrases…

	"I believe…"
or	"I consider…"
or	"I think…"
or	"In my opinion…"

They are endorsing their own recommendation. As a result they should not be surprised when some of the people they seek to influence respond with:

"Well you would say that, wouldn't you?"

The embarrassment associated with having to deal with the *"well you would say that",* response can be avoided if you do the following:

- Provide support to your idea, recommendation or proposal with EVIDENCE of the success it has brought others.

- Provide THIRD PARTY REFERENCES that your contacts respect and who they consider to be similar to themselves, their businesses or the circumstances with which they are faced.

How To
Manage
Effectively

DO YOUR TEAM MEMBERS REALLY KNOW WHAT THEY ARE EXPECTED TO ACHIEVE?

Many companies provide their staff with Job Descriptions which set out the tasks they want an individual to undertake. However, all too few ensure that each task is accompanied by MINIMUM STANDARDS OF PERFORMANCE.

Every employee recognises that their performance is being assessed. But every employee wants the basis of any assessment to be fair and objective. This is where Minimum Standards of Performance (MSOP) are so important.

MSOPs can be NUMERICAL or QUALITATIVE

Numerical standards can include:

- Frequency
- Accuracy
- Time taken
- Monetary results (e.g. Turnover, Profit, Margin)

You should always include Numerical standards within Job Descriptions; because they are specific

Qualitative standards relate to HOW WELL a task is performed. They are far more difficult to establish than numerical. Nonetheless, it is important to define what you consider to be your measurement of "how well" a task is performed.

When seeking to establish qualitative MSOPs consider the actions you expect the job holder to undertake to complete

a task to your minimum satisfaction. Write the MSOPs using such phrases as:

"Is seen to..."
"When there is evidence of..."
"When his actions result in..."

As you create qualitative MSOPs, avoid the trap of using RELATIVE TERMS, such as:

Better	Bigger	Less
Higher	Smaller	Fewer
Lower	Greater	Larger

When you use any of those words the job holder is likely to ask:

"Better than what?"
"Higher than what?"

Job Descriptions which do not contain MSOPs are of very limited value. Therefore aim to set at least three MSOPs for each KEY TASK you include in the Job Descriptions you produce for your team members.

CATCH PEOPLE DOING SOMETHING RIGHT

How many managers think that their job revolves around catching people doing things wrong? I have met a lot. They focus on the "control" element of their job. They monitor every aspect of an employee's performance and appear to gain pleasure from telling that employee:

"That's wrong."
"You should not have done that."
"That didn't work."
"You've got it wrong... again."

Successful managers recognise the importance of monitoring an individual's performance and taking corrective action when necessary. However, they focus far more of their attention on CATCHING PEOPLE DOING SOMETHING RIGHT.

By doing so they create opportunities to MOTIVATE people. This contrasts with the demotivational effect of any form of corrective action.

Positive acknowledgements of what people do right encourages individuals to develop great habits and to look for ways to improve other aspects of their performance.

ARE YOU A "WHAT" OR A "HOW" MANAGER?

The goal of people management is to achieve successful results consistently through others. That involves you becoming a "What" **AND** "How" manager.

Regrettably too many of the managers I have met during my business career are only "WHAT" managers. The "What" manager tells their people what they need to do. They do not show them HOW to achieve any goal.

Of course, it would not be productive to spoon feed your staff with ideas. However, whenever you ask someone to do something new, different, more challenging and demanding you cannot abdicate your responsibility to show your team members HOW to fulfil their responsibility.

Why do so many managers adopt the *"this is what I want you to do"* style, rather than the *"let me show you how to"* style?

The main reason is managers' inner fear of having to DEMONSTRATE a new or different skill. Therefore, follow this process:

1. Test your ability to demonstrate a new skill. Invite a colleague or your boss to provide you with feedback.
2. Analyse what you demonstrated to identify your areas of strength and your competency shortcomings.

3. If the skill you are seeking to demonstrate is a complex one, then record your rehearsal. You may be pleasantly surprised, or concerned, by what you hear.

"WHAT" managers never achieve sustained success, whereas "HOW" managers develop their people to develop their company.

HOW DO YOU COMMUNICATE WITH YOUR TEAM?

When you speak with individuals within your team, or the group as a whole, do the following words feature frequently in your vocabulary:

"I", "ME", "MY"

You may think such phrases as:

> *"I think..."*
> *"I consider..."*
> *"I believe..."*
> *"I feel..."*
> *"The most important thing to me is..."*
> *"If you ask me..."*
> *"In my opinion..."*
> *"My view is..."*
> *"My solution is..."*

are always acceptable to your team members. Rarely is this the case, because you are seeking to impose your views or will on others rather than secure the group or an individual's buy in.

If you replace "I", "Me" and "My" with *"YOU", "WE" or "US"* you will obtain a far more positive response. Look at the examples shown on the next page:

"I think we should ... ..."

(Change to: *"You will all have thoughts on the actions we should take. What are those?"*)

"In my opinion the only way is..."
(Change to: *"What's your opinion on... ?"*)

Management by consultation is far more powerful than management by direction.

DO YOU TELL OR ASK OTHERS?

It's so easy to tell someone what to do. A short, sharp statement will do. However, telling is rarely the most effective way to achieve successful results through others.

When you ASK people to take actions the result can be very effective, provided you ask in the RIGHT way.

Asking involves the use of carefully constructed questions. Look at the examples shown below of the "wrong" and "right" questions:

WRONG	RIGHT
"Can you do that as soon as possible?"	*"By what time can you have that completed?"*
"Do you have the time to do that?"	*"When will you start work on...?"*
"Could you help me?"	*"In what ways would you like to assist me with this project?"*

The right question avoids the "Yes/No" response. It also focuses the recipient on taking specific actions.

ARE YOU TUNED INTO YOUR PEOPLES' FAVOURITE RADIO STATION, W.I.I.F.M.?

As a Manager, Director or Business Owner you spend a great deal of your time conveying information to others. You hold team meetings, you conduct one-to-one discussions, you speak over the phone and you write emails. However, when you are planning how you will convey your points do you always seek to tune into your team member's favourite radio station W.I.I.F.M.

W.I.I.F.M. stands for What's In It For Me.

Successful managers recognise that they cannot please all of the people all of the time. However, even when difficult news has to be conveyed it has to be done in ways which acknowledge that recipients are always concerned about how they will benefit or be disadvantaged by your message.

By the way, don't just associate W.I.I.F.M. with financial rewards or material gains. There are many occasions on which employees are looking for emotional gains; such as involvement, recognition, or being asked for their opinion.

When a radio is not tuned in properly the interference and lack of clarity annoys every listener. It's the same with employees. If you are not tuned into their wavelength, they will register their irritation.

NOTE TAKING – IT ACTS LIKE THE BRAKES ON YOUR CAR

Just how good is your memory? I ask because I have sat through hundreds of business meetings and watched attendees take **NO** notes. Clearly these people were putting their memory to the test.

Whether you are in a business meeting or holding a one-to-one discussion with a team member, you should always be ready to take notes. Note taking acts like the brakes on your car. It slows you down.

Note taking gives you time to think, to evaluate what has been said, to digest information and to consider alternative responses.

Note taking also enables you to restate what others have said to ensure you have interpreted accurately what has been discussed.

ARE YOU THE BIGGEST SOURCE OF DEMOTIVATION WITHIN YOUR COMPANY OR ORGANISATION?

None of us like to think we have a negative influence on our team member's motivation. However, look at the causes of employee irritation and frustration shown below. Could any be applied to you?

1. Fails to give employees recognition for their achievements.
2. Does not provide employees with regular feedback on their performance.
3. Does not stimulate healthy competition within the team.
4. Fails to show a genuine interest in employees.
5. Never delegates effectively... if at all.
6. Demonstrates inconsistent managerial behaviour.
7. Focuses on what people do wrong rather than what they do right.
8. Delivers open reprimands.
9. Breaks promises.
10. Tells rather then asks.

I could have listed many other sources of demotivation. However, my message is, look at every aspect of your behaviour and then ask yourself this question:

"If I was the one receiving this behaviour how would I respond?"

There are many things that can influence the motivation of your team members over which you can exercise little influence. But your behaviour isn't one of those things.

DON'T MOTIVATE YOUR TEAM MEMBERS!

Companies spend millions on initiatives designed to motivate employees. But how effective are these initiatives?

The inherent problem with any form of motivation is that its effects are *TEMPORARY.* They can give an initial boost to productivity and performance, yet rarely is this improvement sustained. That is why I recommend to managers, directors and business owners that they should focus consistent attention on identifying and addressing what DEMOTIVATES their staff.

Some managers are afraid to ask an employee the question: *"What demotivates you?"* For fear of receiving an answer they do not want to hear. But ignorance is not a blissful state.

Once you have identified the factors that demotivate individuals and, as a result, influence their performance, you can determine actions to remove, or at least reduce the effects of, those factors.

So spend less time and money on motivational schemes and more time on understanding and eliminating the negative influences on your people

HELP YOUR PEOPLE TO UNDERSTAND WHAT THE TERM "AMBITION" REALLY EMBRACES

Our society encourages individuals to be *"ambitious"*. But do your team members understand what ambition really embraces?

I define "ambition" in a business context, as *"The desire to take on more RESPONSIBILITY, AUTHORITY and ACCOUNTABILITY, in order to secure higher rewards and recognition"*.

RESPONSIBILITY does not just mean the addition of tasks. It involves undertaking tasks which are of greater importance.

AUTHORITY involves making decisions which have a greater impact or potential consequences.

ACCOUNTABILITY is where the buck stops with the individual, and it's a much larger buck.

The acquisition of more responsibility, authority and accountability can, and often does, increase the emotional pressure on an individual. Hence individuals refer to *"the stress of the job"*.

As managers our role is to help team members, who profess to being ambitious, to understand what can be gained and lost from realising those ambitions.

Unless an individual understands the potential gains and losses, they cannot make a judgement on how far they wish to pursue their ambitions.

ARE THE PEOPLE WHO WORK WITH AND FOR YOU AMBITIOUS OR NOT?

Getting the best out of the people who work with and for you starts with understanding what's important to each person. What are their ambitions? What are their aspirations? What motivates them each day?

The interesting thing is that many employees do not consider these questions in detail until they are prompted.

You can provide that prompt by inviting each of your team members to prepare WRITTEN responses to these questions:

"What do I want to achieve over the course of the next (?) years?"(Let each person set their own time period)
"How will I achieve these goals?"
"By when will I achieve each goal?"
"What could I GAIN from achieving my goals?"
"What could I LOSE from achieving my goals?"

You may think each question is simple to answer. Think again. It takes a great deal of careful thought and dialogue with family and/or friends to determine precise answers.

The act of committing answers to paper is important. It focuses the mind and it identifies how serious an individual is about determining, with help, their future.

When you understand more about your team members' objectives/goals your communication with them will be far more focused and relevant. Without knowledge of your team members' objectives you are far more likely to provide incorrect motivation and this could lead to individuals leaving your employment.

Do you really believe you can work HARDER?

Do you really believe you can work MORE?

Perhaps you can do both. On the other hand it's worth remembering that your job, as a manager, is to achieve successful results consistently through others. You cannot do that without delegating.

WHAT IS DELEGATION?

I define it as:

"Giving another person the AUTHORITY to act on your behalf, for a prescribed period of time, by making them RESPONSIBLE for seeing that a job is done, and holding them ACCOUNTABLE to you for the results achieved.

What do the terms RESPONSIBILITY, AUTHORITY and ACCOUNTABILITY mean?

RESPONSIBILITY:	Means taking ownership and understanding of the job or work you are given to do.
AUTHORITY:	Means the right or power to make decisions and take action.
ACCOUNTABILITY:	Means *"carrying the can"*.

Delegation can only succeed when all three factors are put in place.

WHY IS IT SO IMPORTANT FOR YOU TO DELEGATE?

- There is nothing to be gained from working eighteen hours a day – except ulcers!
- You need to utilise all the skills of your team members.
- Delegation gives you time to plan and think.
- Delegation multiplies your productivity.
- Delegation motivates individuals.
- Delegation encourages individuals' sense of responsibility.

Remember, if you let go, people grow.

TO WHOM SHOULD YOU DELEGATE?

When you are considering delegating part of your job, here are some factors you should take into account when selecting the recipient of your delegation:

- Who has the INTEREST in taking on a new task?
- Who would BENEFIT from additional responsibility?
- Who has the TALENT?
- Who has the TIME?
- How will others react/respond to the person I would like to choose?
- What HELP would the individual need from me to ensure they succeed when fulfilling the delegated task?

HOW TO DELEGATE SUCCESSFULLY

- Identify those tasks, within your job, which could be delegated.
- Invite the person to whom you wish to delegate to accept the task(s).
- Explain the nature of the task(s) and the objective(s) you wish to achieve.
- Provide your selected person with advice on how to fulfil a task, but without restricting their ability to demonstrate their flair and creativity.
- Establish deadlines for the completion of the task(s).
- Confirm your team member's limits of authority and accountability.

If you still consider that delegation is not for you reflect on this saying:

"If you are indispensable you are unpromotable."

HOW OFTEN DOES THE WORD "PROBLEM" FEATURE IN YOUR VOCABULARY?

Management brings you face to face with problems every day. However, it is your attitude that determines how you address each problem. Your challenge is to show the people you manage, and with whom you work, that the difficulties they face can only be resolved by POSITIVE ACTIONS.

When conveying this point delete the word "PROBLEM" from your vocabulary.

Problem is a word that stimulates negative thoughts in many people. Have you ever heard anybody express such statements as:

"We've got a problem," or *"Yet another problem has arisen,"* with a smile on their face?

Replace the word "problem" with one of the following:

"issue", "topic", "subject", "matter"

Each of the words can be expressed in far more positive ways. For example:

"That's an important issue, let's look for a solution," or *"That matter needs addressing. How should we tackle it?"* or *"Let's look at that subject,"* or *"That's definitely a topic for more discussion."*

SOLVE YOUR PROBLEMS BY FOLLOWING MY PECAR© APPROACH

So much of our daily lives are spent dealing with "problems" and, much as we may try to reduce the number we encounter, they never seem to go away.

What's the solution? Well problems cannot be ignored for ever. In addition, when problems occur it is tempting to have the following dialogue with oneself:

"Have I had this problem before? Yes, I have. What did I do last time? I did…. Did it work? Reasonably well. Then I might as well repeat the actions."

Hardly scientific, clinical and objective thinking!

Here's another method that will make your problem solving a more structured process. It's my PECAR© approach.

Step One: Define the PROBLEM.
It's not as easy as you think. Because all too often the definition is confused by effects.

Step Two: Explore all of the EFFECTS of the problem.

Step Three: Identify and isolate the CAUSES.

Step Four: Decide upon the ACTIONS you should take.
Most business related problems require a multiple set of linked actions. Act upon your decisions. Delays can exacerbate a solution.

Step Five: Monitor your RESULTS.
Learn from successes and from those actions you take which do not produce the desired outcome.

HOW DO YOUR TEAM MEMBERS BRING THEIR PROBLEMS TO YOUR ATTENTION?

Many Directors and Managers, with whom I have worked, have said to me:

"My life revolves around solving my team's problems," or, *"You cannot imagine how many problems my team bring me each day."*

Those Directors and Managers often go on to complement themselves on how well, or how fast, they solve their influx of problems. Sadly, the complements are unjustified. Because if you spend your life solving everyone else's problems you will never have time to do your job!

Effective Directors and Managers always advise their team members that they can only bring problems to their Director or Manager's attention **IF** it is accompanied by a proposed SOLUTION.

If you introduce your team members to my P.E.C.A.R.© approach then they can formulate solutions.

Solutions should always be accompanied by a description of the RESULT that is being sought and expected.

DO YOU USE "KILLER PHRASES"?

Great Managers are always conscious communicators. They recognise that just one misplaced or mistimed word can have the most negative effects on relationships. Consequently, they are particularly careful to avoid using KILLER PHRASES.

Take a look at the phrases shown below and reflect upon whether you have used any in the recent past.

> *"It's a good idea, but..."*
> *"We've tried that before..."*
> *"If it is such a good idea why hasn't anyone mentioned it before?"*
> *"That's all right in theory."*
> *"You cannot be serious!"*
> *"That will never work!"*
> *"You haven't thought that through!"*

A KILLER PHRASE is one which kills enthusiasm, destroys ideas and chloroforms creative thinking. If you do not eliminate them from your vocabulary you will find yourself surrounded by people who either wait for your instructions or leave your employment.

ARE YOUR MEETINGS A WASTE OF TIME?

Every week companies spend enormous sums of money running meetings. You may be a manager who has contributed to that expense. But what do your meetings achieve?

If you are going to hold a meeting follow these guidelines:

- Decide upon the specific RESULTS you want to achieve.
- Decide who NEEDS to attend.
- Check their availability.
- Send an AGENDA in advance of the meeting to all attendees.
- Ensure the agenda describes WHAT is to be discussed, WHAT each attendee needs to prepare for the meeting and HOW each attendee will benefit from the meeting.
- Decide upon the STYLE of the meeting. Informal? Highly participative and discussion based? Project led?
- Allocate sufficient time to cover every subject thoroughly.
- Prepare MATERIALS you want attendees to use during, or take away from, the meeting.
- Start on TIME. A late start conveys an impression of casualness and a lack of importance to all attendees.
- Reach ACTION AGREEMENTS when you have covered each item on the agenda. Hold attendees to their action commitments and deliver yours.

Meetings enable you to engage your people in the process that will enable you all to achieve your objectives.

DON'T UNDERTAKE "ANNUAL PERFORMANCE REVIEWS" OR "ANNUAL APPRAISALS"

So many companies put in place systems and procedures for managers to undertake *"annual appraisals"* or *"annual performance reviews"*. But the whole process seems bizarre and totally ridiculous to me.

It's hard enough to remember how someone performed three months ago, let alone a year ago! Besides, if an employee is performing well or poorly they do not want or need to wait a year to have an *"official review"*.

Every employee needs feedback on their performance. But that feedback needs to be frequent and related directly to recent activities.

When you are planning to have a feedback session with a team member ALWAYS invite them to prepare a self-assessment of their performance.

Self-assessments place the onus on an employee to provide evidence of their successes or explanations for why their performance did not reach the standards you both would have wanted.

ACTUALLY I'M NOT AGAINST FORMAL PERFORMANCE REVIEWS

Having been critical of the "Annual Performance Review/Appraisal" let me confirm that I do see merit in formalising employee performance reviews… provided the method used is an objective one.

A Performance Review constitutes a discussion about HOW WELL an individual has performed over a prescribed period of time. The review needs to focus on the ATTITUDES demonstrated by an individual, the KNOWLEDGE they have acquired and demonstrated and the SKILLS they have shown when fulfilling their job.

The trouble with discussions about how well someone has performed is that they can become HIGHLY SUBJECTIVE. Opinions can override facts.

You can reduce the subjectivity by the following actions:

1. Create a list of the Attitudes, Knowledge and Skills you expect your employee to have or demonstrate when undertaking their job.
2. Give your team member the list and ask them to assess their performance, under each heading using my FORCED CHOICE RATING SYSTEM. Your team member should assess their Attitudes, Knowledge and Skills using a NUMERICAL RATING – that of 2,4,6 and 8…

The "4" rating represents the minimum standard of performance you expect an individual to achieve.

The Forced Choice rating does not allow you, or your team member, to choose the soft option of an average rating. You or they are forced to choose the minimum standard of performance (4) or a higher or lower rating.

If you have 40 headings within the job holder's Attitudes, Knowledge and Skills profile you have a potential MSOP of 160.

Remember you can only assess someone's performance if you have seen them undertake their job. If you have not seen your team member demonstrating a specific Attitude, Knowledge or Skill you exclude a rating. For example, if 10 headings out of 40 cannot be assessed the MSOP reduces to 120, and you have an obligation to spend more time with your team member as they undertake their job.

IF YOU DON'T KNOW WHO YOU ARE LOOKING FOR, HOW WILL YOU KNOW YOU'VE FOUND THE RIGHT PERSON?

One of the biggest challenges we face as managers is that of recruiting the right people for our company. Recruitment can be like a minefield in which the explosions occur after we have hired someone. Therefore, let's look at one aspect of the preparatory work you need to undertake for each recruitment campaign.

The effectiveness of any employee can be expressed with this formula:

$E=(A+K+S)\ p$

Effectiveness = Attitude + Knowledge + Skills
        influenced by Personality

Attitude determines how people use the knowledge and skills they have acquired. So write down a list of the Attitudes you require in the job holder you seek, and then write at least one question you will ask to identify if your applicant has each of the desired attitudes.

Ensure your questions are all STRUCTURED. This means they are prefixed by Who, What, Where, When or How and that each question requires the applicant to:

- DEMONSTRATE
- SHOW
- ILLUSTRATE
- DESCRIBE

their attitudes.

Your next task is to write a list of the KNOWLEDGE you expect your future employee to bring to your Company. Examination results and professional qualifications can provide evidence of knowledge gained. ALWAYS ask for proof of claimed qualifications. However, it does not follow that if a prospective employee has KNOWLEDGE they also have the skill to apply it. As you will see on page 71.

HOW GOOD AN INTERVIEWER ARE YOU?

One of the ironies of management is that if you are a great manager your people stay with you. Therefore, you don't need to recruit very often. However, when you don't recruit regularly you can become rusty at interviewing. This can lead to you asking the WRONG questions.

You already know the importance I attach to STRUCTURED QUESTIONING, because I refer to structured questions as the most powerful tool in your communications kit bag. But structured questioning involves far more than just the use of the *"What"*, *"Who"*, *"How"*, *"Where"* and *"When"* prefix. Great interviewers know how to use the right combination of words when they ask a prospective employee questions.

Look at the questions shown below. They are all structured. So what's wrong with each one?

"How enthusiastic are you?"
"What are you like when it comes to managing change?"
"How well do you get on with people?"

Each question lets the applicant say what they want you to hear!

Change the wording and you ensure an applicant has to think very carefully about the response he will give.

On the next page are those earlier questions worded differently:

"How do you demonstrate enthusiasm consistently to your customers?"

"What are the specific actions you take to ensure that any change within your department is undertaken successfully?"

"What are the three most important actions you take to ensure you maintain great relationships with the people with whom you work?"

Applicants often try to conceal opinions, characteristics, personality traits and disappointments they have experienced. You can reveal hidden information by ensuring your questions contain words which require an applicant to show, demonstrate, illustrate, describe and explain.

HOW OFTEN DO YOU TEST THE SKILLS OF THE PEOPLE YOU INTERVIEW FOR ROLES IN YOUR COMPANY?

Part of your planning for a recruitment activity is that of producing a list of the SKILLS you require a job holder to be able to demonstrate. You refine that list by determining the degree of proficiency you require an applicant to possess. But do you also create TESTS that will require an applicant to prove they have the competencies you need?

There should be a test for every skill and you should establish a measurement of proficiency.

Remember, knowledge can be acquired through learning and skills can only be mastered through application.

There are many people who know what to do but who cannot apply that knowledge.

DO YOU UNDERSTAND THE DIFFERENCE BETWEEN "ATTITUDE" AND "PERSONALITY"?

One of the most challenging managerial tasks is that of recruiting staff. There are so many traps into which you can fall when seeking the right person.

One of the most common traps is to confuse ATTITUDES with PERSONALITY.

"Attitude" is a frame of mind. It is how someone feels and thinks at a given point in time. Attitude has a fundamental influence over how someone performs in a job. An individual's attitude is never fixed. It can be changed by a variety of external or internal factors.

"Personality" is the combination of generic traits we have acquired from our relatives. Personality characteristics rarely change.

Attitudes can be identified and confirmed at interviews through highly perceptive questions and through seeking evidence of an applicant's application of an attitude.

Personality traits can be identified through discussion with an applicant's current or past employer.

I appreciate that some employers are reluctant to discuss the performance or personality of past employees. However, the risks associated with making a recruitment decision without knowledge of an individual's personality far outweigh the effort you may need to make to speak with an applicant's previous employer.

70

RIDE THE TRAINING AND DEVELOPMENT CYCLE TO SUCCESS

All of the training you deliver to your team members has to be PLANNED. Objectives need to be set and sufficient time needs to be allocated. Once your planning is complete undertake your training with the following sequence in mind:

EXPLANATION
What the task is

DEMONSTRATION
How the task is done

APPLICATION
Let your team member try
to undertake the task

EXAMINATION
Review, analyse and improve

However competent a person may consider themself to be there will always be new lessons to learn and old habits to discard.

PRACTICE DOES NOT MAKE PERFECT

You will recall the old saying:

"PRACTICE MAKES PERFECT"

I am sure someone has said it to you and you may have said it to your team members. But have you realised that the saying is fundamentally flawed?

If you practice something over and over again, which you do not undertake correctly, then the result is a situation where you are simply increasing the number of occasions on which you make mistakes.

The saying becomes far more relevant if it is amended as follows:

"Practice and ANALYSIS helps to make you perfect."

Therefore, the message is always analyse your own performance, seek analysis from individuals with greater knowledge and skills and provide your team members with guidance on how they can improve and develop.

ROLE PLAYING IS NOT PLAY ACTING

It is rare to find someone who does not want to improve an aspect of their personal or professional performance. That's why so many people welcome training to improve their sporting performance. But when it comes to improving how they perform in their job, many people are highly reluctant to practice new approaches, methods or techniques. Why?

Embarrassment can be a key factor. Individuals consider they will *"show themselves up"* in front of their manager and/or colleagues. You can remove (or at least reduce) individuals' fear of embarrassment if you follow these guidelines:

1. Ensure that all role play activities are related to **REAL** business situations.
2. Explain that role plays allow individuals to:
    -   Push against their "comfort zone" in a low risk environment.
    -   Practice specific techniques.
    -   React spontaneously to situations.
    -   Analyse their own strengths and shortcomings.
3. Ensure each role play is PLANNED. Both the role player and the recipient of the role play need to have a working brief.
4. Ensure the audience for any role play is briefed to provide constructive and specific feedback only.

When people are not given the opportunity to PRACTICE activities and ANALYSE their performance, the outcome of their efforts in real life situations is (invariably) disappointing.

HOW OFTEN DO YOUR TEAM MEMBERS FAIL TO ACT UPON THE TRAINING AND INFORMATION YOU PROVIDE?

Whenever you are conveying new knowledge and skills to a team member, it is essential that you check three key things:

1. Did they UNDERSTAND what you said?
2. Did they ACCEPT what you said?
3. Will they ACTION what you said?

You need to ask carefully constructed questions to address each issue. Here are some examples:

"What is your ATTITUDE towards what we have discussed today?"
"What are your VIEWS on that approach?"
"What is your OPINION on that technique?"
"How will you use that method?"
"In what situations can it be used most effectively?"
"Which type of customer would respond best to that approach?"
"When will you start using that approach?"
"What RESULTS will you target to achieve after adopting that technique?"

When you gain a team member's formal commitment to action what you have proposed, ensure you monitor the results they achieve and provide them with feedback on these outcomes.

74

TEN QUESTIONS USED REGULARLY BY MANAGERS WHO DEVELOP THEIR PEOPLE

1. What's your OPINION?
2. How would you HANDLE THIS MATTER?
3. What would you do if you were ME?
4. What RESULTS would you expect to achieve?
5. What would you do, if it were YOUR MONEY?
6. What CHANGES would you make?
7. What OPTIONS have you considered?
8. WHEN would you take action?
9. What could we GAIN from that approach?
10. What could we LOSE from that approach?

DEVELOP PEOPLE INDIVIDUALLY AS WELL AS COLLECTIVELY

Many of the Chief Executives with whom I have worked have expressed with great pride their commitment to developing their people. They have described the various programmes they have put in place and I will always commend such commitment. However, what is often overlooked, or at least not actioned effectively, is the development of people as INDIVIDUALS rather than just employees.

The imparting of core knowledge and universal skills can be undertaken through group activities. The cultivating of individuals' strengths and elimination of personal shortcomings can only be achieved successfully through PERSONAL COACHING.

PERSONAL COACHING tests every manager's ability to explain and demonstrate new skills to their staff. For this reason it is essential that you allocate time to your own development. Seek help from such sources as management books and articles, on-line features, colleagues and friends. Never be afraid to admit a lack of knowledge or skills. If you do not seek on-going personal development your ability to develop individuals within your team will be restricted. The result of that could be them failing to perform more successfully.

TEN WAYS TO STIMULATE IDEAS AND CREATIVE THINKING WITHIN YOUR TEAM

1. *Invite* your team to challenge the status quo. Remember Einstein's definition of madness: *"Doing the same thing over and over again and expecting a different result."*
2. Delegate – don't abdicate or just give out jobs.
3. Give people the right to make mistakes.
4. Eliminate negative words and phrases from your vocabulary.
5. Be seen to treat obstacles as opportunities.
6. Look for the positives in peoples' ideas and not the potential negatives.
7. Recognise peoples' new ideas – give them credit for their suggestions.
8. Build individuals confidence – remind them that success comes in cans and not can'ts.
9. Evaluate ideas and suggestions promptly.
10. Make a record of your team's *"Success stories"*.

WHAT DOES "JOB SATISFACTION" LOOK LIKE TO YOUR TEAM?

Individuals only develop and grow when they are engaged in activities they WANT to do. Therefore, providing them with the opportunities to undertake such activities is an important aspect of your job as a manager. Your aim should be to enable your team members to gain real JOB SATISFACTION.

Study the statements below to see if you are generating and maintaining job satisfaction for your team members:

- I show a regular and sustained interest in each of my team member's performance.
- I identify and act upon what demotivates my team members.
- I engage people regularly in decision making.
- I invite opinions and views.
- I provide team members with recognition for their achievements.
- I seek to provide my team members with a sense of security at work.
- I encourage team work amongst employees.
- I provide individuals with opportunities to grow and develop.
- I seek to place people in jobs for which they are aptitudinally suited.
- I provide fair but firm supervision.
- I behave consistently towards team members.

GENERATE A "SUCCESS CULTURE" WITHIN YOUR COMPANY

Success can be defined in a variety of ways. However, regardless of the criteria used, it is important for you to generate a "Success Culture" within your organisation.

To achieve that goal introduce your team to ten of the keys to success in business. They are:

1. PERSEVERANCE

   As Thomas Edison said: *"Genius is one per cent inspiration and ninety-nine per cent perspiration."*

2. ACTION

   Make don't wait for things to happen.

3. TRYING THE UNTRIED

   Challenge the status quo. Think the unthinkable.

4. DOING WHAT OTHERS THINK CANNOT BE DONE

5. ELIMINATING NEGATIVE THOUGHTS, WORDS, PHRASES AND BODY LANGUAGE

6. HAVING HIGH EXPECTATIONS

7. ACCEPTING OWNERSHIP

8. ACCEPTING RESPONSIBILITY

9. ACCEPTING ACCOUNTABILITY

10. ACHIEVING CONSISTENCY

Remind your team members that success is always temporary. Past successes do not guarantee future glory. Consistent success comes from looking forward and not backwards. Learn from the past – don't live in it!

DEVELOP YOUR PEOPLE TO MANAGE CHANGE

It has often been said that…

"The only thing constant in life is change".

However, the word "change" has a unique ability to conjure up an immense variety of pictures in the minds of most people. Sadly, too many of those pictures are negative ones. If your team are afraid, or at least wary, of change, then try these actions:

1. Demonstrate to each of your team members that you have an *"open minded"* approach to change.
2. Demonstrate a flexibility in your thinking by always being prepared to listen and evaluate proposed changes.
3. Be prepared for frustrations and disappointments. Look upon disappointments as learning opportunities.
4. Be prepared to reappraise your working methods and effectiveness.
5. Remove all traces of indifference you may have had in the past over the need for change.
6. Demonstrate a desire to acquire new skills.

For your company to develop your people must embrace change. They will only be responsive to change when you are seen to be the architect, implementer and supporter of change.

Show them that the **FEAR** of change is just:

False
Expectations
Appearing
to be **R**eal

DO YOU HAVE A CREATIVE CULTURE IN YOUR COMPANY?

We spend so much of our time DOING things that rarely do we give ourselves enough time to THINK, to muse, to reflect and to open our minds to new ideas and approaches.

I recognise that those day-to-day pressures will not go away. However, those companies that will succeed consistently in the future are the ones that provide their people with the opportunity to be creative.

Two of the most successful ways to stimulate creativity within your company are:

1. Establish INNOVATION GROUPS within your company.
    Innovation Groups comprise four or five employees drawn from different job functions but who share a similar status. The group meets once a month (or every six weeks) to brainstorm and discuss new ideas.

    The group does not discuss how they can change things within the company or within a specific department. Their focus is solely on the creation of something NEW. Their aim is to seek INNOVATION and not imitation.

    Innovation groups should appoint their own chairperson and that individual should be different each time the group meets. I always recommend that innovation groups meet for no more than forty-five minutes. This restricted time focuses the members' minds.

I recommend that innovation groups meet on no more than four occasions before the composition of the group is changed. If the same people meet on more than three/four occasions the freshness of their thinking reduces and the results of their discussions are often disappointing.

2. Establish a *"CREATIVE EMPLOYEE CORRIDOR OF FAME"*

    Your objective is to select a corridor within your building which is a busy traffic route for employees and visitors and within this corridor install photographs of those employees who have created outstanding ideas for the company. The photographs should be accompanied by the name of the employee and details of their idea and the benefits it has brought to the company.

CUSTOMER CARE – IT'S EVERYONE'S AFFAIR

Technology has allowed companies to reduce the differences which exist between products. As a consequence the attitudes, knowledge and skills demonstrated by employees now represent the biggest potential differentiator for every company.

To encourage your team members to deliver consistently high levels of customer care, provide each person with this acronym.

Communication	The initiative must be yours.
Understanding	Always try to see your customer's point of view.
Sincerity	Insincerity always shows through.
Tolerance	It is essential and not merely desirable.
Opportunism	Look for opportunities to build upon your customer relationships.
Motivation	Encourage others to share your motivation for customer care.
Enthusiasm	It is infectious and stimulates business relationships.
Resilience	Bounce back from the inevitable knocks we encounter in business.
Creativity	Look for new ways to improve our organisation, its services and results.
Appearance	Remember, first impressions are important.
Responsiveness	The speed of your response reflects the importance you attach to your customer.
Effectiveness ©	Do the job right and well as do the right job.

DO YOU ENCOURAGE YOUR TEAM MEMBERS TO QUESTION CONSTRUCTIVELY?

I love the saying:

"If you employ a YES man then one of you is redundant."

Businesses thrive when there is a culture in which people are encouraged to question what, how, when and why actions are taken. However, questioning needs to be CONSTRUCTIVE.

Anyone can complain or criticise. It is far more difficult to comment and then provide an effective alternative course of action. Therefore, advise your team members that you want their ideas, observations and feedback provided each comment is accompanied by a recommendation and an anticipated result.

Recommendations need to be specific. This means that they include WHAT should be done, by WHOM, by WHEN and HOW. Results also need to be specific. Comments such as, *"if we do that, things will be better"* and *"changing that will improve things"* provide no indication of the results that could be achieved from taking a different course of action.

Companies in which constructive questioning flourishes are the ones that are focused on the future. Those companies in which questioning is discouraged (or even banned) are destined for failure.

WHAT WOULD YOU DO IF YOU WERE ME?

As every manager knows, employees can be challenging and difficult. They often seek to force you to make action decisions without allowing you time to consider various potential courses of action.

If you respond too quickly to challenges you may make a decision which leads to even more conflict. Therefore, when you are faced with an individual who wants to place you under constant pressure, consider posing this question:

"WHAT WOULD YOU DO IF YOU WERE ME?"

When a difficult employee reflects carefully on the question, they realise that the instant response of *"I would do it"* or *"I would act"* or *"I would agree"* has many dangers.

You are placing your employee in a position where they have to think, reflect, consider alternatives, decide and propose a course of action.

Your question can help them to realise that management is never about shooting from the lip and making instant decisions.

HARNESS THE POWER OF SILENCE

Management involves far more listening than talking. That is because you cannot listen if you are talking incessantly.

I have often thought that the over talkative manager should have a sign put on his desk which says:

W.A.I.T. (Why Am I Talking?)

During conversations silence can be created by the action of you taking notes or such expressions as, *"Let me think about that for a minute"*.

It can also be generated by you inviting your team member or contact to write notes of what has been discussed, reviewed, considered or agreed. Remember, note taking acts like the brakes in your car. It slows down or stops temporarily a conversation.

Ineffective managers often speak because they have to say something. Effective managers only speak when they have something valuable to say.

Remember to always treat silence as your ally and not your enemy. After all, silence has been described as the hardest thing to refute.

DO YOU ALWAYS EXPLAIN WHY YOU WANT SOMETHING DONE?

When you are under pressure to get things done it is all too easy to fall into the trap of giving orders or instructions without explaining WHY you want something done.

The consequences of just giving out orders include:

- You receiving lots of questions.
- Individuals making their own assumptions about your motives.
- Potential conflict.

Therefore, follow these guidelines when you are explaining WHY you want something done:

1. Put yourself in your team member's position. What would you like to know and hear if you were that person?
2. Ensure the reasons you give for making your request are precise.
3. Link your reasons to the outcomes you want achieved from taking the action.
4. As well as explaining what can be gained from taking the action you require you can also highlight what could be lost if action is not taken.

WHAT SHOULD BE MY NEXT MOVE?

This is a question that many of the people who have worked for me have asked. They were thinking about gaining promotion and with it associated benefits. I always responded to their question with my own:

"WHAT DO YOU ENJOY DOING?"

My question has often surprised individuals because I believe they expected specific advice or at least a recommendation. Promotion, in the business world, involves taking on more RESPONSIBILITY, more AUTHORITY and more ACCOUNTABILITY. All three can bring material benefits. They can also generate more stress. That's why I have always encouraged my team members to focus on what they enjoy doing.

When you enjoy activities you put more energy into their completion, you demonstrate more commitment and you achieve more success.

As your team members consider their next move, encourage them to look at roles which will deliver emotional benefits first and material rewards second.

HOW DO YOU COUNSEL YOUR TEAM MEMBERS WHEN SOMETHING GOES WRONG?

Employees can be great workers. However, they can also be unreliable, inconsistent, casual, lazy and a hundred and one other negative things... all because they are human!

Managing people means you have to deal with negative, as well as the positive, aspects of individuals' behaviour.

There are numerous traps into which you can fall when you address individuals' shortcomings. Here are some guidelines on how to avoid many of the traps:

- When a performance and/or behavioural shortcoming takes place your first task is to ensure your team member recognises, and understands, that there is a problem.
- When an individual fails, or chooses not to recognise the problem, you have to create the awareness by raising the subject by means of an indirect approach.
- Prior to any counselling session prepare the structured questions you need or wish to ask that will enable the individual to recognise his or her shortcomings.
- Rehearse your opening to the discussion.
- Be prepared to take time over bringing your team member to an awareness of the nature and extent of their shortcomings.

- Once your team member acknowledges there is an issue to address invite them to give their assessment of the EFFECTS of their actions.
- Progress your discussion by inviting your team member to talk about the CAUSES of the situation.
- Encourage them to propose a SOLUTION.
- Invite them to draw up an ACTION PLAN.
- Remain positive and supportive throughout the discussion.

Counselling always takes time. It cannot be rushed. Be prepared to show patience.

HOW SHOULD YOU CORRECT SOMEONE WHEN COUNSELLING HAS NOT PRODUCED THE POSITIVE OUTCOME YOU SOUGHT?

Wouldn't it be great if every time we were called upon to counsel a team member we achieved a positive outcome? Sadly life is never that simple.

Changing peoples' behaviour and performance can take a lot of time and many discussions. You will find yourself having to take CORRECTIVE action at some point in your managerial career. When you do follow this approach:

- Make certain you have as many **FACTS** as possible to hand. You should not be dealing with allegations, assertions, assumptions, rumours or hearsay.
- Meet your team member in a private location.
- Do not enter a corrective discussion with a set course of action in mind. Remain prepared to hear your team member's point of view.
- Invite your team member to give their assessment of the situation.
- Seek agreement on what you both consider to be the causes of the problem.
- Highlight the advantages of early corrective action.
- Develop a joint Action Plan.
- Confirm a date and time for your next meeting.

YOU CANNOT MANAGE TIME

I have always been fascinated by those managers who tell me they are "great at time management". My fascination stems from the fact that you cannot manage time. You can only manage your use of it.

Time cannot be bought, sold, borrowed, stolen, retrieved, saved, manufactured, reproduced or modified. But it can be WASTED.

Here are ten tips to help you use your business time wisely:

1. Don't put off until tomorrow what you could and should do today. Because "tomorrow" is a mystical land where ninety per cent of all productivity, motivation and success is stored.

2. When scheduling your work divide your task list into those that are PROFIT/INCOME GENERATING and those that are COST ACTIVITIES.

3. Establish your PRIORITIES on the basis of is each task IMPORTANT, URGENT or both.

4. Tell people when you are available, so they know when you are not accessible.

5. Find the "off" button on your mobile phone and use it.

6. Don't look upon the number of emails you receive each day as a measure of your importance.

7. Follow the *"do it to the finish"* and *"handle it just once"* approach to all your work.

8. Don't create very long "to do" lists. It is not how many activities you have completed in a day that's important. It is what has resulted from those you have undertaken.

9. Delegate regularly.

10. PLAN every activity. Without a PLAN you could be on a Path Leading Absolutely Nowhere.

DO YOU KNOW THE DIFFERENCE BETWEEN "EFFICIENT" AND "EFFECTIVE"?

Have you noticed how frequently the words *"efficient"* and *"effective"* are used during business meetings? Whenever I hear the words I wonder if the users really understood their meaning.

For me the words have very different meanings. Here are my definitions:

EFFICIENT: Doing the job right

EFFECTIVE: Doing the right job

Of course your aim has to be both efficient and effective. However, it is very easy to focus on being efficient and not realise that you are not being effective.

Achieving effectiveness starts with you asking yourself such questions as:

"Does this task need to be undertaken?"
"Do I need to undertake this task?"
"How important is this task?"
"How urgent is this task?"

When you make a habit of asking yourself these questions you soon realise that, whilst it is important to do jobs right, it is far more important to ensure you start with the right job.

Who is Philip Cripps?

Philip is widely regarded as one of the leading authorities on communication and management skills. He has written for publications across the world and speaks frequently at major conferences. He is CEO of Thameside International, the UK's foremost people development consultancy, which has a fifty-year record of success.

Philip is no desk jockey – he spends a great deal of his time coaching and developing people in their work places. He delivers coaching that delivers outstanding results... consistently.

Find out more about how to communicate more successfully and manage more effectively by contacting me

Philipc@thamesideinternational.com

Lightning Source UK Ltd.
Milton Keynes UK
UKOW07f0052261117
313323UK00008B/38/P